797,885 Books

are available to read at

Forgotten Books

www.ForgottenBooks.com

Forgotten Books' App
Available for mobile, tablet & eReader

ISBN 978-1-330-64689-2
PIBN 10086993

This book is a reproduction of an important historical work. Forgotten Books uses state-of-the-art technology to digitally reconstruct the work, preserving the original format whilst repairing imperfections present in the aged copy. In rare cases, an imperfection in the original, such as a blemish or missing page, may be replicated in our edition. We do, however, repair the vast majority of imperfections successfully; any imperfections that remain are intentionally left to preserve the state of such historical works.

Forgotten Books is a registered trademark of FB &c Ltd.
Copyright © 2015 FB &c Ltd.
FB &c Ltd, Dalton House, 60 Windsor Avenue, London, SW19 2RR.
Company number 08720141. Registered in England and Wales.

For support please visit www.forgottenbooks.com

1 MONTH OF FREE READING

at

www.ForgottenBooks.com

By purchasing this book you are eligible for one month membership to ForgottenBooks.com, giving you unlimited access to our entire collection of over 700,000 titles via our web site and mobile apps.

To claim your free month visit:
www.forgottenbooks.com/free86993

* Offer is valid for 45 days from date of purchase. Terms and conditions apply.

English
Français
Deutsche
Italiano
Español
Português

www.forgottenbooks.com

Mythology Photography **Fiction**
Fishing Christianity **Art** Cooking
Essays Buddhism Freemasonry
Medicine **Biology** Music **Ancient Egypt** Evolution Carpentry Physics
Dance Geology **Mathematics** Fitness
Shakespeare **Folklore** Yoga Marketing
Confidence Immortality Biographies
Poetry **Psychology** Witchcraft
Electronics Chemistry History **Law**
Accounting **Philosophy** Anthropology
Alchemy Drama Quantum Mechanics
Atheism Sexual Health **Ancient History**
Entrepreneurship Languages Sport
Paleontology Needlework Islam
Metaphysics Investment Archaeology
Parenting Statistics Criminology
Motivational

BYZANTINE HISTORY IN THE EARLY MIDDLE AGES

3721 B35

BYZANTINE HISTORY

IN THE

EARLY MIDDLE AGES

THE REDE LECTURE
DELIVERED IN THE SENATE HOUSE, CAMBRIDGE
JUNE 12, 1900

BY

FREDERIC HARRISON, M.A.
HONORARY FELLOW, WADHAM COLLEGE, OXFORD

London
MACMILLAN AND CO., Limited
NEW YORK: THE MACMILLAN COMPANY
1900

3/10/01

~~3721 B35~~

A.151288

BYZANTINE HISTORY IN THE EARLY MIDDLE AGES

In one of the most suggestive of his essays, Professor Freeman calls the Roman Empire on the Bosphorus "the surest witness to the unity of history."[1] And Professor Bury, whose great work has done so much to develop that truth, insists that the old Roman Empire did not cease to exist until the year 1453, when Mohammed the Conqueror stormed Constantinople. The line of Roman emperors, he says, "continued in unbroken succession from Octavius Augustus to Constantine Palaeologus."[2] Since George Finlay, nearly fifty years ago, first urged this truth on public attention, all competent historians have recognised the continuity of the civilisation which Constantine seated on the Golden Horn; and they have done justice to its many services to the West as well as to the East.[3] But the nature of that continuity, the extent of these services, are still but dimly understood by the general public. Prejudice, bigotry, and rhetoric have done much to warp the popular conception of one of the chief keys to general history. In spite of all that scholars have said, the old sophism lingers on that the empire and civilisation of Rome ended with Romulus Augustulus in 476, until, in a sense, it was revived by the great Charles; that, in the meanwhile, a vicious and decaying parody of the Empire eked out its contemptible life on the Bosphorus.

Such was the language of the popular writers of the last century, and Gibbon himself did something to encourage this view. When, in his 48th chapter, he talked of Byzantine annals as "a tedious and uniform tale of weakness and misery," and saw that he still had more than eight centuries of the history of the world to compress into his last two volumes, we suspect that the great master of description was beginning to feel exhausted by his gigantic task.[4] In any case, his undervaluing Byzantine history as a whole is the main philosophical weakness of his magnificent work of art. The phrases of Voltaire, Le Beau, and of papal controversialists still linger in the public mind;[5] and in the meantime there exists no adequate history in English of the whole course of the Roman Empire on the Bosphorus. This still forms the great *lacuna* in our historical literature.

Modern historians continually warn their readers to cast off the obsolete fallacy that a gulf of so-called dark ages separates ancient from modern history; that ancient history closes with the settlement of the Goths in Rome, whilst modern history mysteriously emerges somewhere in the ninth or the tenth century. We all know now that, when the northern races settled in Western Europe, they assimilated much that they inherited from Rome. In truth, the Roman Empire, transplanted on to the Bosphorus, maintained for many centuries an unbroken sequence of imperial life; retaining, transforming, and in part even developing, the administrative system, the law, the literature, the arts of war, the industry, the commerce, which had once been concentrated by the Cæsars in Italy. After all the researches of Finlay, Freeman, Bryce, Hodgkin, Bury, Fisher, Oman, Dill, to say nothing of a crowd of French, German, Italian, and Russian specialists, we must regard these facts as amongst the truisms of general history.

The continuity of government and civilisation in the Empire of New Rome was far more real than it was in Western Europe. New Rome never suffered such abrupt breaks, dislocations, such changes of local seat, of titular and official form, of language, race, law, and manners, as marked the re-settlement of Western Europe. For eleven centuries Constantinople remained the continuous seat of an imperial Christian government, during nine centuries of which its administrative sequence was hardly broken. For nine centuries, until the piratical raid of the Crusaders, Constantinople preserved Christendom, industry, the machinery of government, and civilisation, from successive torrents of barbarians. For seven centuries it protected Europe from the premature invasions of the Crescent; giving very much in the meantime to the East, receiving very much from the East, and acting as the intellectual and industrial clearing-house between Europe and Asia. For at least five centuries, from the age of Justinian, it was the nurse of the arts, of manufacture, commerce, and literature, to Western Europe, where all these were still in the making. And it was the direct and immediate source of civilisation, whether secular or religious, to the whole of Eastern Europe, from the Baltic to the Ionian Sea.

In picturesque and impressive incidents, in memorable events and dominant characters, in martial achievement and in heroic endurance, perhaps even in sociologic lessons, Byzantine history from the first Constantine to the last is as rich as the contemporary history either of the West or of the East. It would be a paradox to compare the great Charles, or the great Otto, or our own blameless Alfred, with even the best of the Byzantine rulers of their age, or to place such men as Gregory the Great, or Popes Silvester or Hildebrand, below even the best of the Patriarchs of the Holy Wisdom. Nor have the Orthodox Church or the Eastern Romans such claims on the gratitude of mankind as are due to the Church Catholic and the Teutonic heroes who founded modern Europe. But the three centuries of Byzantine history from the rise of the Isaurian dynasty in 717 down to the last of the Basilian emperors in 1028, will be found as well worthy of study as the same three centuries in Western Europe, *i.e.* from the age of Charles Martel to that of Henry the Saint.

During those three centuries at least, the eighth, ninth, and tenth, the Emperors of New Rome ruled over a settled State which, if not as powerful in arms, was far more rich in various resources, more cultured, more truly modern, than any other in Western Europe. I am not about to attempt, in the short space at my disposal, even a brief sketch of these three centuries of crowded story. I purpose only to touch on some of the special features of its civilisation and culture, which, for the three centuries so often called the darkest ages of Europe, made Constantinople the wonder and envy of the world. Byzantine history has its epochs of ebb and flow, of decay, convulsion, anarchy, and recovery, as had the empire at Old Rome. This Roman Empire was the most continuous institution in Europe, next after the Catholic Church; and, like the Church, it had the same marvellous recuperative energy. It is true that it had none of the latent power of growth which Frank, Lombard, Burgundian, and Saxon possessed. It was from first to last a conservative, tenacious, and more or less stationary force. But it kept alive the principles of order, stability, and continuity, in things material and in things intellectual, when all around it, on the east and on the west, was racked with the throes of new birth or tossed in a weltering chaos. Byzantine story is stained red with blood, is black with vice, is disfigured with accumulated waste and horror — but what story of the eighth, ninth, and tenth centuries is not so disfigured and stained? And even the atrocities of Constantinople may be matched in the history of the Papacy in these very ages, and in the intrigues and conspiracies which raged around the thrones of Frank, Lombard, Burgundian, and Goth.

Strangely enough, the inner life of this Byzantine history has yet to be opened to the English reader. For these three centuries that I am treating, Finlay has given us about 400 pages;[6] and Finlay, alas, is no longer abreast of modern authorities, and was writing, let us remember, the history of Greece. Mr. Bury's fine history stops short as yet with Irene at the end of the eighth century, and Dr. Hodgkin has drawn rein at the same date. For the period I am treating, we have but a hundred pages or so in Mr. Bury's second volume, and the mordant epigrams of Gibbon are about of equal bulk.[7] For the law, the literature, the economics, the administration, the ceremonial, the art, the trade, the manners, the theology of this epoch we have to depend on a mass of foreign monographs,—French, German, Greek, and now Russian and American,—on Rambaud, Schlumberger, Labarte, Bayet, Zachariae, Krumbacher, Heimbach, Krause, Neander, Salzenberg, Huebsch, Kondakov, De Vogüé, Bordier, Texier, Hergenröther, Heyd, Fr. Michel, Silvestre, Didron, Mortreuil, Duchesne, Paspates, Buzantios, Van Millingen, Frothingham.[8] So far as I know, we have not a single English study on the special developments of civilisation on the Bosphorus from the fourth to the twelfth century. Here are a score of monographs open to the research of English historians.

Current misconceptions of Byzantine history mainly arise from inattention to the enormous period it covers, and to the wide differences which mark the various epochs and dynasties. The whole period from the first Constantine to the last is about equal to the period from Romulus to Theodosius. The Crusaders' raid, in 1204, utterly ruined Constantinople, and from that time till the capture by the Turks it was a feeble wreck.⁹ Even at the date of the First Crusade, about a century earlier, the Empire had been broken by the campaign of Manzikert; so that the lively pictures of the First Crusade by Scott and Gibbon present us with the State in an age of decadence.¹⁰ The epoch when Byzantium was in the van of civilisation, civil, military, and intellectual, stretches from the reign of Justinian (527) to the death of Constantine VIII. (1028), a period of exactly five centuries—more than the whole period of the Roman Republic.

During those five centuries there were a series of alternate periods of splendour, decline, revival, expansion, and final dissolution. The rulers differ from each other as widely as Trajan differs from Nero or Honorius; the times differ as widely as the age of Augustus differs from the ages of Cato or of Theodoric. There were ages of marvellous recovery under Justinian, again under Heraclius, again under Leo the Isaurian, then under Basil of Macedon, next under Nicephorus Phocas, and lastly under Basil II., the slayer of the Bulgarians. There were ages of decay and confusion under the successors of Heraclius, and under those of Irene, and again those of Constantine VIII. But the period to which I desire to fix attention is that from the rise of the Isaurian dynasty (717) to the death of Basil II. (1025), rather more than three centuries. During the eighth, ninth, and tenth centuries the Roman Empire on the Bosphorus was far the most stable and cultured power in the world, and on its existence hung the future of civilisation.

Its power was due to this — that for some five

centuries of the early Middle Ages which form the transition from polytheism to feudalism, the main inheritance of civilisation, practical and intellectual, was kept in continuous and undisturbed vitality in the empire centred round the Propontis—that during all this epoch, elsewhere one of continual subversion and confusion, the southern and eastern coast of Italy, Greece and its islands, Thrace, Macedonia, and Asia Minor as far as the Upper Euphrates, were practically safe and peaceful. This great tract, then the most populous, industrious, and civilised of the world, was able to give itself to wealth, art, and thought, whilst East and West were swept with wars of barbarous invaders. The administration of the Empire, its military and civil organisation, remained continuous and effective in the same seat, under the same law, language, and religion, during the whole period; and the official system worked under all changes of dynasty as a single organic machine. It was thus able to accumulate enormous resources of money and material, and to equip and discipline great regular armies from the martial races of its complex realm, such as were wholly beyond the means of the transitory and ever shifting kingdoms in the rest of Europe and Asia.[11]

Western Europe, no doubt, bore within its bosom the seeds of a far greater world to come, a more virile youth, greater heroes and chiefs. But wealth, organisation, knowledge, for the time were safeguarded behind the walls of Byzantium—to speak roughly, from the age of Justinian to that of the Crusades. Not only did this empire of New Rome possess the wealth, industry, and knowledge, but it had almost exclusive control of Mediterranean commerce, undisputed supremacy of the seas, paramount financial power, and the monopoly of all the more refined manufactures and arts. In the middle of the tenth century, the contrast between the kingdom of Otto the Great and the empire of Constantine Porphyrogenitus was as great as that between Russia under Peter the Great and France in the days of the Orleans Regency.[12]

From the seventh to the thirteenth century Constantinople was far the largest, wealthiest, most splendid city in Europe. It was in every sense a new Rome. And, if it were at all inferior as a whole to what its mother was in the palmy age of Trajan and Hadrian, it far surpassed the old Rome in its exquisite situation, in its mighty fortifications, and in the beauty of its central palace and church.[13] A long succession of poets and topographers have recounted the glories of the great city—its churches, palaces, baths, forum, hippodrome, columns, porticoes, statues, theatres, hospitals, reservoirs, aqueducts, monasteries, and cemeteries.[14] All accounts of early travellers from the West relate with wonder the splendour and wealth of the imperial city. "These riches and buildings were equalled nowhere in the world," says the Jew Benjamin of Tudela in the twelfth century. "Over all the land there are burghs, castles, and country towns, the one upon the other without interval," says the Saga of King Sigurd, fifty years earlier. The Crusaders, who despised the Greeks of the now decayed empire, were awed at the sight of their city; and as the pirates of the Fifth Crusade sailed up the Propontis they began to wonder at their own temerity in attacking so vast a fortress.[15]

The dominant note of all observers who reached Constantinople from the North or the West, at least down to the eleventh century, even when they most despised the effeminacy and servility of its Greek inhabitants, was this: they felt themselves in presence of a civilisation more complex and organised than any extant. It was akin to the awe felt by Goths and Franks when they first fell under the spell of Rome. At the close of the sixth century, as Dr. Hodgkin notes of Childebert's fourth invasion of Italy, "mighty were a few courteous words from the great Roman Emperor to the barbarian king"—the king whom Maurice the "Imperator semper Augustus" condescends to address as "vir gloriosus."[16] And this idea that New Rome was the centre of the civilised world, that Western sovereigns were not their equals, lasted down to the age of Charles. When the Caroline Empire was decaying and convulsed, the same idea took fresh force. And the sense that the Byzantine world had a fulness and a culture which they had not, persisted until the Crusades effectually broke the spell.[17]

This sentiment was based on two very real facts. The first was that New Rome prolonged no little of the tradition, civil and military organisation, wealth, art, and literature of the older Rome, indeed far more than remained west of the Adriatic. The second, the more important, and the only one on which I now desire to enlarge, was that, in many essentials of civilisation, it was more modern than the nascent nations of the West. Throughout the early centuries of the Middle Ages— we may say from the age of Justinian to that of Hildebrand—the empire on the Bosphorus perfected an administrative service, a hierarchy of dignities and offices, a monetary and fiscal system, a code of diplomatic formulas, a scientific body of civil law, an imperial fleet, engines of war, fortifications, and resources of maritime mobilisation, such as were not to be seen in Western kingdoms till the close of the Middle Ages, and which were gradually adopted or imitated in the West. At a time when Charles, or Capet, or Otto were welding into order their rude peoples, the traveller who reached the Bosphorus found most of the institutions and habits of life such as we associate with the great cities of much later epochs. He would find a regular city police, organised bodies of municipal workmen, public parks, hospitals, orphanages, schools of law, science, and medicine, theatrical and spectacular amusements, immense factories, sumptuous palaces, and a life which recalls the Cinque Cento in Italy.[18]

It is quite true that this imperial administration was despotic, that much of the art was lifeless and all the literature jejune; that cruelty, vice, corruption, and superstition were flagrant and constant, just as the European Renascence had cruelty, vice, and corruption at the very heart of its culture. The older historians are too fond of comparing the Leos and Constantines with the Scipios and the Antonines, instead of comparing them with the Lombard, Frank, or Bulgarian chiefs of their own times. And we are all too much given to judge the Byzantines of the eighth, ninth, and tenth centuries by the moral standards of our own age; to denounce their pompous ceremonials, their servile etiquette, their frigid compositions, and their savage executions. We forget that for many centuries Western chiefs vied with each other in copying and parading the external paraphernalia of the Roman emperors in their Byzantine ceremonial: their crowns, sceptres, coins, titles, palaces, international usages, golden bulls, pragmatic sanctions, and court officialdom. There is hardly a single symbol or form or office dear to the monarchies and aristocracies of Europe of which the original model was not elaborated in the Sacred Palace beside the Golden Horn. And most of these symbols and offices are still amongst the most venerable insignia to-day at the State functions of Tsar, Kaiser, Pope, and King.[19]

The cohesive force of the Byzantine monarchy resided in its elaborate administration, civil and military. It formed a colossal bureaucracy centred round the sacred person of the Sovereign Lord of so many races, such diverse provinces, such populous towns, united by nothing but one supreme tie of allegiance. No doubt it was semi-Oriental, it was absolutist, it was oppressive, it was theocratic. But for some seven centuries it held together a vast and thriving empire, and for four centuries more it kept in being the image and memory of empire. And with all its evils and tyranny, it was closely copied by every bureaucratic absolutism in modern Europe. And even to-day the *chinovnik* of Russia, the *Beamten* of Prussia, and the *administration* of France trace their offices and even their titles to the types of the Byzantine official hierarchy.

Much more is this true of ceremonial, titles, and places of dignity. We may say that the entire nomenclature of monarchic courts and honours is derived direct from Byzantine originals, ever since Clovis was proud to call himself *Consul* and *Augustus*, and to receive a diadem from Anastasius, and ever since Charles accepted the style of Emperor and Augustus, pacific, crowned of God in the Basilica of S. Peter on Christmas Day, 800 ; when the Roman people shouted "Life and Victory," just as the Byzantines used to do.[20] When in the tenth century our Edward the elder was styled *Rex invictissimus* and Athelstan called himself *Basileus of the English*, they simply borrowed the Greek formulas of supreme rank. We are amused and bewildered, as we read Constantine the seventh on the *Ceremonies of the Court*, by the endless succession of officials, obeisances, compliments, gesticulations, and robings which he so solemnly describes : with his great chamberlain, his high steward, his chief butler, his privy seal, his gold stick, his master of the horse, lords and ladies in waiting, right honourables, ushers, grooms, and gentlemen of the guard. But we usually forget that the Bourbons, the Hapsburgs, Hohenzollerns, and Romanoffs have maintained these very forms and dignities for centuries. Indeed, it might be amusing to take the Purple King's βασίλεια τάξις to a court drawing-room, and check off the offices and forms which still survive after a thousand years. Michael Psellos, in the eleventh century, speaks of his ἥλιος βασιλεύς—the exact equivalent of Louis' *Roi-Soleil*. The officialdom and ceremonial of Byzantium was rotten and absurd enough; but it is not for the courtiers of Europe to scoff at it. It was an anticipation by many centuries of much that we still call civilisation.

And it would be quite wrong to assume that the organisation of the Empire was a rigid and unchanging system. On the contrary, it steadily developed and was recast according to the necessities of the case. In the main, these necessities were the shrinkage of the boundaries, the loss of rich provinces, and, above all, the pressure of Oriental invaders together with the growth of the western kingdoms and empire. Nor was there anything casual or arbitrary in these changes. The process of Orientation and of Autocracy which Aurelian and Diocletian had begun in the third century had been developed into a system by Constantine when he planted the Empire on the Bosphorus and founded an administrative and social hierarchy in the fourth century. Justinian in the sixth century introduced changes which gave the empire a more military and more centralised form to meet the enemies by which it was surrounded. Heraclius and his dynasty in the seventh century carried this process still further under the tremendous strain to which their rule was exposed. They instituted the system of *Themes*, military governorships under a general having plenary authority both in peace and war; and the system of *Themes* was developed, in the eighth and ninth century, until in the tenth they are classified by Constantine Porphyrogenitus, who mentions about thirty. During the whole period, from the seventh to the eleventh centuries inclusive, the organisation was continually developed or varied, not violently or improvidently, but to meet the needs of the time. There is reason to believe these developments to have been systematic, continuous, and judicious. If we compare them with the convulsions, anarchy, racial and political revolutions which shook Western Europe during the same epoch, we cannot deny that the tyrannies and formalities of the Byzantine Court were compatible with high aptitude for Imperial government, order, and defence.[21] Alone amongst the nations of the world, the Empire maintained a systematic finance and exchequer, a pure standard coinage, and a regular commercial marine.

For the historian, the point of interest in this Byzantine administration is that, with all its crimes and pomposities, it was systematic and continuous. It never suffered the administrative and financial chaos which afflicted the West in the fifth century, or in the ninth century after the decay of the Carlings, and so on down to the revival of the Holy Roman Empire by Otto the Great. It is difficult to overrate the ultimate importance of the acceptance by Charles of the title of Emperor, or of its revival by Otto; and history has taken a new life since the modern school has worked out all that these meant to the West. But we must be careful not to fall into the opposite pitfall, as if the Roman Empire had been *translated* back again to the West, as some clerical enthusiasts pretended, as if the Empire of Charles was a continuous and growing organism from the time of Charles down to Rudolph of

Hapsburg, or as if the coronation of Charles or of Otto at Rome broke the continuity of Empire at the Bosphorus, or even greatly diminished its authority and prestige. On the contrary, these Western ceremonies affected it only for a season, and from time to time, and affected its temper more than its power.

The Western Empire, for all the strong men who at times wielded its sceptre, and for the fitful bursts of force it displayed, was long before it quite recognised its own dignity and might; it was very vaguely and variously understood at first by its composite parts; and for the earlier centuries was a loose, troubled, and migratory symbol of rank rather than a fixed and recognised system of government. All this time the Emperors in the vermilion buskins were regularly crowned in the Holy Wisdom; they all worshipped there, and all lived and ruled under its shadow. Their palaces by the Bosphorus maintained, under every dynasty and through every century, the same vast bureaucratic machine, and organised from the same centre the same armies and fleets; they supported the same churches, libraries, monasteries, schools, and spectacles, without the break of a day, however much Muslim invaders plundered or occupied their Asiatic provinces, and although the rulers of Franks or Saxons defied their authority or borrowed their titles. The Empire of Franks and Teutons was not a systematic government and had no local seat. That of the Greeks, as they were called, had all the characters of a fixed capital and of a continuous State system.

There is nothing in all history more astonishing and

more worthy of study than the continual rallies of this Roman Empire. There is an alternate ebb and flow in the extent and power of the Empire most fascinating to observe. The wonderful revival under Justinian, and again that under Heraclius in the sixth and seventh centuries, are familiar enough even to the general reader, as well as the troubles which supervened under their respective successors. The more splendid and more permanent rally under the Isaurian dynasty and again under the Basilian dynasty, the whole period from 717 for three centuries, to the last of the Basilian Emperors, in 1028, is less familiar to English readers, and yet is rich with incidents as well as lessons. The anarchy which followed the fall of the miserable tyrant Justinian II. seemed certain to ruin the whole Empire. From this fate it was saved by the Isaurian (or Syrian), Leo III. and his descendants and successors; and again order and empire were saved by Basil I. of Macedon and his descendants, who ruled for 160 years. The onward sweep of the conquering Muslims had roused the whole Empire to defend its existence. And all through the eighth, ninth, and tenth centuries it found a succession of statesmen and warriors from Asia Minor and Thrace whose policy and exploits at least equal any recorded in the same age either in the East or the West. And it is to be noted that these two glorious periods of the Byzantine power coincided with the great revival of the Franks under Pippin and his dynasty, and that of the Saxons under Henry the Fowler and the dynasty of Ottos.

Nothing could have saved the Empire but its

superiority in war—at least in defence. And this superiority it possessed from the sixth to the eleventh century. It was a strange error of the older historians, into which Gibbon himself fell, that the Byzantine armies were wanting in courage, discipline, and organisation. On the contrary, during all the early Middle Ages they were the only really scientific army in the world. They revolutionised the art of war, both in theory and practice, and in some points brought it to a stage which was only reached in quite modern times, as for instance in mobilisation and in providing ambulance corps. They quite recast the old Roman methods and armies, whilst retaining the discipline, spirit, and thoroughness of Rome. The great changes were fourfold: (1) they made it as of old a native army of Roman subjects, not of foreign allies or mercenaries; (2) they made its main force cavalry, in lieu of infantry; (3) they changed the weapons to bow and lance instead of sword and javelin—and greatly developed body armour; (4) they substituted a composite and flexible army-corps for the old legion. Men of all races were enlisted, save Greeks and Latins. The main strength came from the races of the highlands of Anatolia and Armenia—the races which defended Plevna.

When, towards the close of the fourth century, the battle of Adrianople rang the knell of Roman infantry, the Byzantine warriors organised an army of mounted bowmen. Belisarius and Narses won their victories with ἱπποτοξόται. The cataphracti, or mail-clad horsemen, armed with bow, broadsword, and lance, who formed nearly half the Byzantine armies, were immensely superior both in mobility, in range, and in force to any troops of old Rome, and they were more than a match for any similar troopers that Asia or Europe could put into the field. From the sixth to the tenth centuries we have still extant scientific treatises on the art of war under the names of Maurice, Leo, and Nicephorus. When to this we take into account the massive system of fortification developed at Constantinople, the various forms of Greek fire, their engines to project combustible liquids, and one form that seems the basis of gunpowder, and last of all the command of the sea, and a powerful service of transports and ships of war, we need not doubt Mr. Oman's conclusion that the Byzantine Empire had the most efficient forces then extant, nor need we wonder how it was that for eight centuries it kept at bay such a host of dangerous foes.[22]

The sea-power of the Empire came later, for the control of the Mediterranean was not challenged until the Saracens took to the sea. But from the seventh to the eleventh centuries (and mainly in the ninth and tenth) the Empire developed a powerful marine of war galleys, cruisers, and transports. The war galleys or *dromonds,* with two banks of oars, carried 300 men each, the cruisers 100, and many of them were fitted with fighting towers and machines for hurling explosives and liquid combustibles. Hand grenades, and apparently guns whence gunpowder shot forth fire-balls but not bullets, were their armament. When Nicephorus Phocas recovered Crete from the Saracens, we are told that his expedition numbered 3300 ships of war and transports, and carried infantry, bowmen, and cavalry, a siege train, and engines, in all amounting to 40,000 or 50,000 men.[23] Nothing in the tenth century could rival such a sea power. He might fairly boast as Emperor to the envoy of Otto that he could lay any coast town of Italy in ashes. Such was the maritime ascendency of Byzantium, until it passed in the eleventh century to the Italian republics.[24]

The most signal evidence of the superior civilisation of Byzantium down to the tenth century, is found in the fact that alone of all states it maintained a continuous, scientific, and even progressive system of law. Whilst the *Corpus Juris* died down in the West under the successive invasions of the Northern nations, at least so far as governments and official study was concerned, it continued under the Emperors in the East to be the law of the State, to be expounded in translations, commentaries, and handbooks, to be regularly taught in schools of law, and still more to be developed in a Christian and modern sense.[25] It was the brilliant proof of Savigny that Roman law was never utterly extinct in Europe, and then rediscovered in the twelfth century. As he showed, it lingered on without official recognition amongst Latin subject races in a casual way, until what Savigny himself calls the Revival of the Civil Law at Bologna in the twelfth century.[26] But for official and practical purposes, the *Corpus Juris* of Justinian was superseded for six centuries by the various laws of the Teutonic conquerors. These laws, whatever their interest, were rude prescriptions to serve the time, without order, method, or permanence, the sure evidence of a low civilisation—as Paulus Diaconus said *tempora fuere barbarica.* If we take the Code of Rothari the Lombard, in the seventh century, or the Capitularies of the Carolines, or Saxon Dooms, or the *Liber Papiensis* of the eleventh century, civil law in any systematic sense was unknown in Western Europe, and the *Corpus Juris* was obsolete.[27]

Now, there was no revival of Roman Law in Byzantium, because there it never was extinct. Justinian's later legislation was promulgated in Greek, and his *Corpus Juris* was at once translated, summarised, and abridged in the East. Although schools of law existed in Constantinople and elsewhere, the seventh century, in its disasters and confusion, let the civil law fall to a low ebb. But the Isaurian dynasty, in the age of the Frank King Pippin, made efforts to restore and to develop the law. The *Ecloga* of Leo III. and Constantine V. was promulgated to revise the law of persons in a Christian sense. It was part of the attempt of the Iconoclasts to form a moral reform in a Puritan spirit. This was followed by three special codes—(1) A maritime code, of the Rhodian law, as to loss at sea and commercial risks; (2) a military code or law martial; (3) a rural code to regulate the police of country populations. And a register of births for males was instituted throughout the Empire at the same time.

In the ninth century the Basilian dynasty issued a new legislation which, whilst professing to restore the *Corpus Juris* of Justinian, practically accepted much of the moral reforms of the Isaurians. The *Procheiron* was a manual designed to give a general knowledge of the entire *Corpus Juris* of Justinian. It was followed by the *Epanagoge*, a revision of the *Procheiron*, which was partly the work of that prodigy of learning, the Patriarch Photius. We have other institutional works and a *Peira* or manual of practice, or the application of law to life. But the great work of the Basilian dynasty was the *Basilica*, in sixty books, of Basil I. and Leo VI., the Philosopher, about 890, an epoch that Mr. Bryce justly calls "the nadir of order and civilisation" in the West, at the time when the Carolines ended with Charles the Fat and Lewis the Child. The *Basilica*, which fill six quarto volumes, stood on a par with the *Corpus Juris* of Justinian. It was a systematic attempt to compile a complete code of law, based on the Roman law, but largely reforming it from the influences of Christianity, humanity, and the advancing habits of a new society.

We thus have in Greek a new *Corpus Juris*, a long series of institutions, amendments, text-books, scholiasts, and glosses, down to the foundation at Constantinople of a new school of law by Constantine Monomachus in the middle of the eleventh century, so that the continuity of civil law from Tribonian to Photius and Theophilus the Younger is complete. As Mr. Roby has pointed out (Int. p. ccliii.), these Greek translations and comments are of great value in determining the texts of the Latin originals. The *Basilica*, indeed, was as permanent as the *Corpus Juris*, and has formed the basis of civil law to the Christian communities of the East, as it is to this day of the Greeks. Nor is it worthy of attention only for its continuity and its permanence. It is a real advance on the old law of Rome from a Christian and modern sense. The *Basilica* opens with a fine proem, which is an admirable and just criticism of the *Corpus Juris*. "Justinian," says Basil, "had four codes. We combine the whole law in *one*. We omit and amend as we go on, and have collected the whole in sixty books." [28] The influence of Christianity and its working on personal law was feeble enough in the code of Justinian. The Isaurian and Basilian laws are deeply marked by the great change. They proclaim the principle and work it out to its conclusions—that "there is no half measure between marriage and celibacy." Concubinage disappears and immoral unions become penal. The marriage of slaves is gradually recognised, and the public evidence of marriage is steadily defined. The law of divorce is put very much on the basis of our existing conditions. The wife is gradually raised to equality of rights. She becomes the guardian of her children; women can legally adopt; there can be no tutelage of minors during the life of *either* parent. The property of husband and wife is placed under just conditions, the *patria potestas* is abolished in the old Roman sense, and the succession on death of either spouse is subject to new regulations. The cumbrous number of witnesses to a testament is reduced; the old formal distinctions between personal and real property are abolished, and a scheme of liquidated damages is introduced. There is no feudal system of any kind. There is a systematic effort to protect the peasant from the δυνατοί, to give the cultivator "fixity of tenure."

Here, then, we have proof that the grand scheme of Roman law, which was officially ignored and forgotten in the whole West for six centuries, was continuously studied, taught, and developed by Byzantines without a single interruption, until it was moulded by Christian morality and modern sentiment to approach the form in which the civil law is now in use in Europe. No higher evidence could be found to show that civilisation, morality, and learning were carried on for those troubled times in the Greek world with a vigour and a continuity that have no counterpart in Latin and Teutonic Europe. Strangely enough, this striking fact was ignored till lately by civilians, and is still ignored by our English jurists. The learning on the Græco-Roman law between Justinian and the school of Bologna is entirely confined to foreign scholars; and I have not noticed anything but brief incidental notices of their labours in the works of any English lawyer. It is a virgin soil that lies open to the plough of any inquiring student of law.

Turn to the history of Art. Here, again, it must be said that from the fifth to the eleventh century the Byzantine and Eastern world preserved the traditions, and led the development of art in all its modes. We are now free of the ancient fallacy that Art was drowned beneath the waves of the Teutonic invaders, until many centuries later it slowly came to life in Italy and then north of the Alps. The truth is that the noblest and most essential of the arts—that of building—some of the minor arts of decoration and ornament, and the art of music, down to the invention of Guido of Arezzo in the eleventh century, lived on and made new departures, whilst most of the arts of form died down under the combined forces of barbarian convulsions and religious asceticism. And it was Byzantium which was the centre of the new architecture and the new decoration, whilst it kept alive such seeds of the arts of form as could be saved through the rudeness and the fanaticism of the early Middle Ages. To the age of Justinian we owe one of the greatest steps ever taken by man in the art of building. The great Church of the Holy Wisdom exerted over architecture a wider influence than can be positively claimed for any single edifice in the history of the arts. We trace enormous ramifications of its example in the whole East and the whole of the West, at Ravenna, Kief, Venice, Aachen, Palermo, Thessalonica, Cairo, Syria, Persia, and Delhi. And with all the enthusiasm we must feel for the Parthenon and the Pantheon, for Amiens and Chartres, I must profess my personal conviction that the interior of Agia Sophia is the grandest in the world, and certainly that one which offers the soundest basis for the architecture of the future.[29]

The great impulse given to all subsequent building by Anthemius and Isodorus lay in the perfect combination of the dome on the grandest scale with massive tiers of arches rising from colossal columns—the union of unrivalled engineering skill with exquisite ornament, the whole being a masterpiece of subtlety, sublimity, harmony, and reserve. It is true that the Pantheon, which we now know to be of the age of Hadrian, not of Augustus, and the vast *caldaria* of the Thermæ, had given the earliest type of the true dome.[30] It is true that the wonderful artifice of crowning the column with the arch in lieu of architrave was invented some centuries earlier. But the union of dome, on the grandest scale and in infinite variety, with arched ranges of columns in rows and in tiers—this was the unique triumph of Byzantine art, and nothing in the history of building has borne a fruit so rich. Ravenna, Torcello, St. Mark's, and Monreale are copies of Byzantine churches. Aachen, as Freeman recognises, is a direct copy of Ravenna, from whence Charles obtained ornaments for his palace chapel. And on both sides of the Rhine were constant copies from the city of the great Charles. It is quite true that French, Rhenish, Russian, Moorish, and Saracen architects developed, and in their façades, towers, and exteriors, much improved on the Byzantine type, which, except in Italy, was not directly copied. But the type, the original conception, was in all cases derived from the Bosphorus.

Without entering on the vexed problem of the mode and extent of the direct imitation of Byzantine architecture either in the East or the West, we must conclude, if we carefully examine the buildings in Greece and the Levant, in Armenia and Syria, and on the shores of Italy, that the Bosphorus became the *nidus* of a building art which had a profound influence on Asia and Europe from the sixth to the twelfth centuries. And when justice is done to its constructive science, to its versatility, and at the same time to its severe taste and dignity, this Byzantine type is one of the most masculine and generative forms of art ever produced by human genius. The Holy Wisdom is twice the age of the Gothic cathedrals, and it will long outlive them. In beauty of material it far surpasses them, and if it has been outvied in mass by the mighty temples of the Renaissance, it far exceeds these in richness, in subtlety, and in refinement.[31]

The people who evolved a noble and creative type of architecture could not be dead to art. But even in the arts of form we rate the Byzantines too low. From the sixth to the eleventh century Western Europe drew from Byzantium its type of ornament in every kind. This was often indirectly and perhaps unconsciously done, and usually with great modifications. But all careful study of the mosaics, the metal work, the ivories, the embroideries, the carvings, the coins, the paintings, and the manuscripts of these ages establishes the priority and the originality of the Byzantine arts of decoration.[32] It is undoubted that the art of mosaic ornament had its source there. Mosaic, with its Greek name, was introduced into the ancient world from the East by Greece. But the exquisite art of wall decoration by glass mosaic which we are now reviving was a strictly Byzantine art, and from the fifth to the twelfth century was carried into Europe by the direct assistance of the Byzantine school. The rigid conservatism of the Church, and the gradual decline of taste, stereotyped and at last destroyed the art; but there still exist in Constantinople and in Greece glass mosaic figures as grand as anything in the decorative art of any age.[33]

In the end superstition and immobility more or less stifled the growth of all the minor arts at Byzantium, as confusion and barbarism submerged them in the West. What remnants remained between the age of Justinian and the age of the Normans were nursed beside the

Bosphorus. The art of carving ivory certainly survived, and in the plaques and caskets which are spared we can trace from time to time a skill which, if it have wholly degenerated from Græco-Roman art, was superior to any we can discover in the West till the rise of the Pisan school. The noble Angel of our own museum, the Veroli casket of South Kensington, and some plaques, diptychs, oliphants, vases, and book-covers, remain to prove that all through these early times Byzantine decoration dominated in Europe, and occasionally could produce a piece which seemed to anticipate good Gothic and Renaissance work.[34]

It is the same in the art of illuminating manuscripts. Painting, no doubt, declined more rapidly than any other art under the combined forces of barbarism and the gospel. But from the fifth to the eleventh century the paintings in Greek manuscripts are far superior to those of Western Europe. The Irish and Caroline schools developed a style of fine calligraphy and ingenious borders and initials. But their figures are curiously inferior to those of the Byzantine painters, who evidently kept their borderings subdued so as not to interfere with their figures. Conservatism and superstition smothered and eventually killed the art of painting, as it did the art of sculpture, in the East. But there are a few rare manuscripts in Venice, in the Vatican, the French Bibliothèque Nationale—all certainly executed for Basil I., Nicephorus, and Basil II. in the ninth and tenth centuries—which in drawing, even of the nude, in composition, in expression, in grandeur of colour and effect, are not equalled until we reach the fourteenth century in Europe. The Vatican, the Venice, and the Paris examples, in my opinion, have never been surpassed.[35]

The manufacture of silks and embroidered satins was almost a Greek monopoly all through the Middle Ages. Mediæval literature is full of the splendid silks of Constantinople, of the robes and exquisite brocades which kings and princes were eager to obtain. We hear of the robe of a Greek senator which had 600 figures picturing the entire life of Christ. Costly stuffs and utensils bore Greek names and lettering down to the middle of the fifteenth century. *Samite* is Greek for six-threaded stuff. Cendal is σινδών, a kind of muslin or taffetas. And some exquisite fragments of embroidered robes of Greek work are preserved in the Vatican and many Northern museums and sacristies. The diadems, sceptres, thrones, robes, coins, and jewels of the early Mediæval princes were all Greek in type, and usually Byzantine in origin. So that Mr. Frothingham, in the *American Journal of Archæology* (1894), does not hesitate to write: "The debt to Byzantium is undoubtedly immense; the difficulty consists in ascertaining what amount of originality can properly be claimed for the Western arts, industries, and institutions during the early Middle Ages." [36]

We err also if we have nothing but contempt for the Byzantine intellectual movement in the early Middle Ages. It is disparaged for two reasons—first, that we do not take account of the only period when it was invaluable, from the eighth to the eleventh centuries; and, secondly, because the Greek in which it was expressed falls off so cruelly from the classical tongue we love. But review the priceless services of this semi-barbarous literature when literature was dormant in the West. How much poetry, philosophy, or science was there in Western Europe between Gregory the Great and Lanfranc? A few ballads, annals, and homilies of merit, but quite limited to their narrow localities. For the preservation of the language, literature, philosophy, and science of Greece mankind were dependent on the Roman Empire in the East, until the Saracens and Persians received and transmitted the inheritance.

From the time of Proclus in the fifth century, there had never been wanting a succession of students of the philosophers of Greece; and it is certain that for some centuries the books and the tradition of Plato and Aristotle were preserved to the world in the schools of Alexandria, Athens, and then of Byzantium. Of the study and development of the civil law we have already spoken. And the same succession was maintained in physical science. Both geometry and astronomy were kept alive, though not advanced. The immortal architects of the *Holy Wisdom* were scientific mathematicians, and wrote works on Mechanics. The mathematician Leo, in the middle of the ninth century, lectured on Geometry in the Church of the Forty Martyrs at Constantinople, and he wrote an essay on Euclid, when there was little demand for science in the West, in the age of Lewis the Pious and the descendants of Ecgbert. In the tenth century we have an essay on a treatise of Hero on practical geometry. And Michael Psellus in the eleventh century, the "Prince of Philosophers," wrote, amongst other things, on mathematics and astronomy. From the fourth to the eleventh century we have a regular series of writers on medicine, and systematic treatises on the healing art.

On other physical sciences — Zoology, Botany, Mineralogy, and Geography—a series of Greek writers and treatises are recorded which partly survive in text or in summaries. I need hardly add that I do not pretend to have studied these works, nor do I suppose that they are worth study, or of any present value whatever. I am relying on the learned historian of Byzantine literature, Krumbacher, who has devoted 1200 pages of close print to these middle Greek authors, and on other biographical and literary histories. The point of interest to the historian is not the absolute value of these forgotten books. It is the fact that down to the age of the Crusades a real, even if feeble, sequence of thinkers was maintained in the Eastern Empire to keep alive the thought and knowledge of the ancient world whilst the Western nations were submerged in revolution and struggles of life or death. Our tendency is to confine to too special and definite an era the influence of Greek on European thought, if we limit it to what is called the Renascence after the capture of Constantinople by the Turks. In truth, from the fifth century to the fifteenth there was a gradual Renascence, or rather an infiltration of ideas, knowledge, and art, from the Grecised Empire into Western Europe. It was never quite inactive, and was fitful and irregular, but in a real way continuous. Its effect was concealed and misrepresented by national antipathies, commercial rivalries, and the bitter jealousies of the two Empires and the two Churches. The main occasions of this infiltration from East to West were undoubtedly — first, the Iconoclast persecutions, then the Crusades, and finally the capture of the City by Mohammed the Conqueror. The latter, which we call the Renascence, may have been the more important of the three, but we must not ignore the real effect of the other two, nor the constant influence of a more advanced and more settled civilisation upon a civilisation which was passing out of barbarism through convulsions into order and life.[37]

The peculiar, indispensable service of Byzantine literature was the preservation of the language, philology, and archaeology of Greece. It is impossible to see how our knowledge of ancient literature or civilisation could have been recovered if Constantinople had not nursed through the early Middle Ages the vast accumulations of Greek learning in the schools of Alexandria, Athens, and Asia Minor; if Photius, Suidas, Eustathius, Tzetzes, and the Scholiasts had not poured out their lexicons, anecdotes, and commentaries; if the *Corpus Scriptorum historiae Byzantinae* had never been compiled; if indefatigable copyists had not toiled in multiplying the texts of ancient Greece. Pedantic, dull, blundering as they are too often, they are indispensable. We pick precious truths and knowledge out of their garrulities and stupidities, for they preserve what otherwise would have been lost for ever. It is no paradox that their very merit to us is that they were never either original or brilliant. Their genius, indeed, would have been our loss. Dunces and pedants as they were, they servilely repeated the words of the immortals. Had they not done so, the immortals would have died long ago.[88]

Of the vast product of the theology of the East it is impossible here to speak. As in the West, and even more than in the West, the intellect of the age was absorbed in spiritual problems and divine mysteries. The amount of its intellectual energy and its moral enthusiasm was as great in the East as in the West; and if the general result is so inferior, the reason is to be found not in less subtlety or industry in the Greek-speaking divines, but rather in the lower social conditions and the rigid absolutism under which they worked. From the first, the Greek Church was half Oriental, profoundly mystical and metaphysical. But we can never depreciate that Orthodox Church which had its Chrysostom, its Cyril and Methodius, the Patriarch Photius, and Gregory of Nazianzus, with crowds of preachers, martyrs, and saints; which, in any case, was the elder brother, guide, and teacher for ages of the Church Catholic; which avoided some of the worst errors, most furious conflicts, the grossest scandals of the Papacy; and which brought within its fold those vast peoples of Eastern Europe which the Roman communion failed to reach.[89]

The Greek Church, which never attained the centralisation of the Church of Rome, was spared some of those sources of despotism and corruption which ultimately tore the Western Church in twain. And, if it never became so potent a spiritual force as was Rome at its highest, in the Greek Church permanent conflict with the Empire and struggles for temporal dominion were unknown. The Greek Church, however, had its own desperate convulsions in the long and fierce battle between Iconoclasts and Iconodules. It would be a fatal error to undervalue this great and significant schism as if it were a mere affair of the use of images in worship. Iconoclasm was one of the great religious movements in the world's history—akin to Arianism, to the Albigensian heresies of the thirteenth century, akin to Mahometanism, akin to Lutheranism, akin to some forms of Puritanism, though quite distinct from all of these. It was evidently a bold and enthusiastic effort of Asiatic Christians to free the European Christians of the common Empire from the fetichism, idol-worship, and monkery in which their life was being stifled.

The Isaurian chiefs had the support of the great magnates of Asia Minor, of the mountaineers of Anatolia, and the bulk of the hardy veterans of the camp. Their zeal to force on a superstitious populace and on swarms of endowed orders of ecclesiastics a moral and spiritual reformation towards a simpler and more abstract Theism —to purge Christianity, in fact, of its grosser anthropomorphism—this is one of the most interesting problems in all history. And all the more that it was a moral and spiritual reform attempted, not by poor zealots from the depths of the popular conscience, but by absolute sovereigns and unflinching governments, which united something of the creed of the Waldenses to the cruel passions of Simon de Montfort. The movement showed how ready was the Asiatic portion of the Empire to accept some form of Islam; and we can well conceive how it came that Leo III. was called σαρακηνόφρων, "imbued with the temperament of an Arab." The whole story has been shamelessly perverted by religious bigotry, and we know little of Iconoclasm, except in the satires of their enemies the Iconodules. One of the greatest rulers of the Empire has been stamped with a disgusting nickname, and it is difficult now to discover what is the truth about the entire dynasty and movement. Mr. Bury has given us an admirable chapter on this remarkable reformation of faith and manners. But we need a full history of a very obscure and obstinate conflict which for a century and a half shook the Empire to its foundations, severed the Orthodox Church from the Church Catholic, and yet greatly stimulated the intercourse of ideas and arts between the East and the West.[40]

In pleading for a more systematic study of Byzantine history and civilisation in the early Middle Ages, I am far from pretending that it can enter into rivalry with that of Western Europe. I do not doubt that it was a lower type; that neither in State nor in Church, neither in policy nor in arms, in morals, in literature, or in art, did it in the sum equal or even approach the Catholic Feudalism of the West. And assuredly, as the West from the time of Charles and Otto onwards rose into modern life, Eastern Christendom sank slowly down into decay and ruin. My point is simply that this Byzantine history and civilisation have been unduly depreciated and unfairly neglected. And this is especially true of English scholars, who have done little indeed of late in a field wherein foreign scholars have done much. It is a field where much remains to be done in order to redress the prejudices and the ignorance of ages, multiplied by clerical bigotry, race insolence, and the unscrupulous avarice of trade. Hardly any other field of history has been so widely distorted and so ignorantly disparaged.

Let me also add that it is for a quite limited period of the thousand years of Byzantine history that I find its peculiar importance. The Justinian and Heraclian periods have brilliant episodes and some great men. But the truly fertile period of Byzantine history, in its contrast with and reaction upon the West, lies in the period from the rise of the Isaurian to the close of the Basilian dynasty—roughly speaking, for the eighth, ninth, tenth, and first half of the eleventh centuries. The Isaurian dynasty undoubtedly opened a new era in the Empire; and in some respects the Basilian dynasty did the same. If we limit our field further, we might take the Macedonian period, where our authorities are fuller, from the accession of Basil I. to the death of Basil II. This century and a half may fairly be compared with the same epoch in the East or in the West. By the middle of the eleventh century, when the Basilian dynasty ended, great changes were setting in, both in the East and the West. The rise of the Seljuks and of the Normans, the growth of Italian commerce, the decay of the Eastern Empire, the struggles of the Papacy and the Western Empire, and finally the Crusades, introduce a new World. It is the point at which Byzantine history loses all its special value for the problems of historical continuity and comparison. And yet it is the point at which a new colour and piquancy is too often given to Byzantine annals.

In the eighth, ninth, and tenth centuries we may trace a civilisation around the Bosphorus which, with all its evils and the seeds of disease within it, was in one sense far older than any other in Europe, in another sense, was far more modern; which preserved things of priceless value to the human race; which finally disproved the fallacy that there had ever been any prolonged break in human evolution; which was the mother and the model of secular churches and mighty kingdoms in Eastern Europe, churches and kingdoms which are still not willing to allow any superiority to the West, either in the region of State organisation or of spiritual faith.[41]

NOTES

NOTES

[1] Freeman, *Historical Essays*, third series, 1879, p. 241.—This essay was a composite embodiment of a series of reviews, beginning with one in 1855 on Finlay's earlier volumes, and incorporating much later matter. It is one of the most eloquent and impressive of all Professor Freeman's writings, and has exercised a deserved influence over English historical thought. It is entitled "The Byzantine Empire," to which name Mr. Bury has shown very valid objections. Mr. Bury's own style, "The Later Roman Empire," serves his purpose in his work, the period of which is from Arcadius and Honorius to Irene, *i.e.* from A.D. 395 to 802. But it is not adequate as a description of the Empire from the foundation of Constantinople to its capture by the Turks. The only accurate name for this is the "Empire of New Rome," which covers the eleven centuries from the first Constantine to the last. Whilst prejudice remains so strong it may be as well to avoid the term "Byzantine Empire," though Mr. Oman has not hesitated to use it as his title. But it is inevitable to speak of Byzantine history, or art, or civilisation, when we refer to that which had its seat on the Bosphorus.

[2] J. B. Bury, *The Later Roman Empire*, vol. i. preface, p. 5.—This masterly work is the most important history of the Eastern Empire from the fifth to the opening of the ninth century that has appeared since Gibbon, and is more full and more modern than the corresponding part of Finlay's work. Mr. Bury has had the great advantage of access to all that has been done in the last fifty years by German, French, Russian, Hungarian, Greek, and Oriental scholars, who have added so greatly to the materials possessed by Gibbon, or even by Finlay. It is to be hoped that Mr. Bury will

be induced to continue his work at least down to the Crusades. He has already thrown light on the period in his notes and appendices to his edition of Gibbon's *Decline and Fall* (7 vols., Methuen), now happily at last complete. And in the *English Historical Review*, vol. iv. 1889, he has given us a valuable sketch of the eleventh-century emperors. It is unfortunate that, as his work rests at present, Mr. Bury has not treated the Basilian dynasty, A.D. 867-1057, the two centuries when the Empire was at the height of its brilliancy and fame—the period when it was most deserving of study.

[3] George Finlay's *History of Greece from* B.C. 146 *to* A.D. 1864, first began in 1843, completed by the author and revised by him in 1863, was finally edited by H. F. Tozer, in seven volumes, for the Clarendon Press, 1877. In speaking of this fine work, one must use the hackneyed and misused word that it created an epoch, at least for English readers. But it has to be borne in mind that Byzantine history was not the direct subject of Finlay's labours, and that the Empire of New Rome occupies at most the first three of Finlay's seven volumes, or about one hundred pages to a century. And the parts of Gibbon directly occupied with Constantinople and its rulers form no larger proportion of the whole work. Yet Gibbon and Finlay still remain the only English historians who have treated systematically the continuous story of the eleven centuries from the first Constantine to the last. The general reader may get some notion of this period from Mr. Oman's pleasant summary in the "Story of the Nations" series—*The Byzantine Empire* (Fisher Unwin, 1892).

[4] Gibbon's *Decline and Fall*, ed. J. B. Bury, vol. v. pp. 169-174. [Mr. Bury's new edition of Gibbon is quoted in these notes.]

[5] Voltaire's famous remark about Byzantine history as "a worthless repertory of declamation and miracles, disgraceful to the human mind," has drawn down the indignation of Finlay, vol. ii. p. 8, and of Bury, vol. i. p. 6. How often, indeed, did Voltaire himself find the same faults in the annals of the West and of Christian Rome! Mr. Lecky would no doubt hardly now write of the "universal verdict of history," what he incidentally dropped out more than thirty years ago in his *History of European Morals*, ii. p. 13.

Lebeau's *Histoire du Bas-Empire*, 1756-79, 22 vols., which

nobody now reads, has given the Empire of New Rome a label which modern learning has not yet been able to scrape off. It is one of those unlucky books of which nothing survives but the title, and that is a blunder and a libel. Lebeau did for the Roman Empire of the Bosphorus what Iconodules did for Constantine V. He gave it an ugly nickname—which sticks.

As to the bitter contests between the theologians of Old and of New Rome, good summaries may be found in Neander's *Church History*, third period, sect. iv. 2, 3; fourth period, sect. 2, 3, 4; and also in Milman's *Latin Christianity*, vol. ii. bk. iv. ch. 6, 7, 8, 9, 12; vol. iii. bk. vii. ch. 6; see also Neale, Rev. J. M., *Holy Eastern Church*.

[6] Gibbon's ch. xlviii. sketches Byzantine history from A.D. 641 to 1185, *i.e.* five centuries (in 70 pp. of the new edition by Bury, vol. v.) In ch. xlix. he treats Iconoclasm; and in ch. liii. he returns to the tenth century for some general reflections.

J. B. Bury's *Later Roman Empire*, vol. ii. bk. vi., deals with the eighth century. His work closes with the fall of Irene, 802.

Dr. Hodgkin, *Italy and Her Invaders*, vol. viii., closes the work with the coronation of Charles as Emperor in 800, and a short account of the close of his reign.

[7] Finlay, for the entire period down to the capture by the Turks, and Bury down to the end of the seventh century, have incidentally treated of the economics, art, manners, and literature of the Byzantine world. Mr. Bury also in his notes and appendices to his edition of Gibbon has given most valuable special summaries and references to later authorities. Mr. Bryce's *Holy Roman Empire*; Mr. Herbert Fisher's *Mediæval Empire*, 2 vols. 1898; Mr. Tout's *Empire and the Papacy*, 918-1273, have very useful notices of Byzantine history, and Mr. Charles Oman's *History of the Art of War*, 1898, has valuable chapters, bk. iv., on the Byzantine warfare from A.D. 579 to 1204.

[8] As to recent monographs on special features of Byzantine history, the following may be consulted:—

I. Administration and Economics

T. H. Krause, *Die Byzantiner des Mittelalters in ihrem Staats-, Hof- und Privatleben*, 1869.—A review of the military, civil, social, and religious organisation of the Empire from the tenth to the fourteenth centuries from Byzantine sources.

RAMBAUD, *L'Empire Grec au Xme Siécle*, 1870.—The life and reign of Constantine Porphyrogenitus.

HEYD (Wilhelm von), *Histoire du Commerce du Levant au Moyen Age*, ed. Fr. 1885.

SCHLUMBERGER, *Un Empereur Byzantin, Nicephorus Phocas*, 1890; *L'Epopée Byzantine, Basil II.*, 1896; *Sigillographie de l'Empire Byzantin*, 1884.

SABATIER, *Monnaies Byzantines*, 1862.

II. LAW

ZACHARIAE VON LINGENTHAL (C.E.), *Collectio Librorum Juris Graeco-Romani ineditorum*, etc., Leipsic, 1852; *Jus Graeco-Romanum*, 1856; *Histoire du Droit Graeco-Romain*, translated by E. Lauth, Paris, 1870.

MORTREUIL (Jean A. B.), *Histoire du droit Byzantin*, 2 vols., Paris, 1843.

MONFERRATUS (A. G.), *Ecloga Leonis III. et Constantini*, 1889.

HEIMBACH, *Basilicorum Libri LX.*, 1833-70, ed. by Zachariae von Lingenthal, 6 vols. 4to.

HAUBOLD, C. G., *Manuale Basilicorum*, 1819. 4to.

III. LITERATURE

KRUMBACHER, Carl, *Geschichte der Byzantinischen Literatur*, 1897.

HERGENRÖTTER (Cardinal), *Photius*, 1867-69, 3 vols. 8vo.

IV. ART

BAYET (Ch.), *L'Art Byzantin*, new edition, 1892.
CORROYER (Edouard), *L'Architecture Romaine*.
FERGUSON, *History of Architecture*, 1874.
TEXIER, *Asie Mineure*.
TEXIER AND PULLAN, *Byzantine Architecture*, 1860.
DE VOGÜÉ, *Les Eglises de Terre Sainte*, 1860; *Architecture Civile et Religieuse de la Syrie*, Paris, 1866-77.
HUEBSCH (trad. Guerber), *Monuments de l'Architecture Chrétienne*, Paris, 1866.

V. ANTIQUITIES

DIDRON, *Annales Archéologiques*, 1844-81; *Iconographie Chrétienne*, 1843, 4to; *Manuel d'Iconographie Chrétienne*, 1845.

LABARTE, *Histoire des Arts Industriels au Moyen Age*, 1864; *Le Palais Impérial de Constantinople*, 1861, 4to.

SALZENBERG, *Alt-christliche Baudenkmale*, 1854, fol.

PASPATES, Βυζαντινὰ Ἀνάκτορα, 1885; Βυζαντιναὶ Μελέται, 1877.

AGINCOURT (J. Seroux de), *Histoire de l'Art par les Monuments*, 6 vols. fol. 1822.

RUSKIN, *Stones of Venice*.

DIEHL (Charles), *L'Art Byzantin dans l'Italie Méridionale*, Paris, 1894; *Études d'Archéologie Byzantine*, 1877.

DURAND (Julien), *Trésor de San Marc*, Paris, 1862.

KONDAKOV (Nic. Partovich), *Histoire de l'Art Byzantin*, Paris, 1886.

MICHEL (Francisque), *Recherches sur la commerce des étoffes de soie, etc.*, Paris, 1862.

SILVESTRE, *Paléographie Universelle*, Paris, 1841.

SILVESTRE ET CHAMPOLLION, *Universal Palæography*.

WESTWOOD, *Palæographia Sacra Pictoria*.

N. HUMPHREYS, *Illuminated Books of the Middle Ages*.

W. MASKELL, *Ivories in South Kensington Museum*; *Russian Art in South Kensington Museum*.

PROF. A. VAN MILLINGEN, *Byzantine Constantinople, its Walls and Sites*, 1899.

A. L. FROTHINGHAM, *Byzantine Artists in Italy*, American Journal of Archæology, 1894-95.

[9] The story is well told in the excellent volume by Mr. Pears, a barrister resident in Constantinople and practising in the local courts. *The Fall of Constantinople in the Fourth Crusade*, by Edwin Pears, LL.D., 1885.

See also Riant, *Exuviæ sacræ Constantin.*, 1887; Hopf, *Chroniques Gréco-Romaines inédites*.

The Crusaders' raid and the sack of Constantinople was one of the most wanton crimes of the Middle Ages, and remains the great opprobrium of the thirteenth century and of Innocent III. Far more destruction was caused to the antiquities of the city by these pretended Crusaders than by the Turks at their conquest. Invaluable records of the ancient world perished therein.

[10] Mr. Oman, in his *Art of War in the Middle Ages*, 1898, bk. iv. ch. iv., "Decline of the Byzantine Army (A.D. 1071-1204)," has well explained the collapse of the Empire consequent on the battle of Manzikert, 1071, when Alp-Arslan, at the head of the

Seljuks, defeated Romanus Diogenes. Manzikert was the Cannæ, or rather the Zama of the Empire, and if any battle deserves so to be called, was one of the decisive battles of the world. It is singular how many great revolutions in the history of the world were collected close around that date of 1071. As Mr. Bury truly says: "The eleventh century was the turning-point of the Middle Ages" (*English Historical Review*, iv. 41, 1889).

[11] Mr. Bury, in his *Later Roman Empire*, and in the Appendices to his *Gibbon*, has given us most valuable pictures of the mighty bureaucracy which was the real source of strength of the Byzantine government, both civil and military. Finlay's second volume tells the same story. Consult also Rambaud's *L'Empire Grèc au Xme Siècle*, which gives an elaborate picture of the administration; also Krause's *Byzantiner des Mittelalters*; Oman's *Art of War* (bk. iv.) and Schlumberger's various works *u.s.* It must be remembered that the organisation of the empire was not at all immutable, but was frequently modified under new conditions. But it was *organic*, *i.e.*, invariably centred round the one head permanently seated in Constantinople, and it was practically *continuous* under all changes of dynasty and palace revolutions. This from the seventh to the tenth centuries made almost the difference between a civilised state and tribes in process of settlement.

[12] Consult Bury, Appendix 5 to *Gibbon*, vol. vi. p. 538, on the Byzantine Navy; also Schlumberger's *Nicephorus Phocas*, ch. ii.; Krause *u.s.*, 265-274; and Gfrörer, *Byzantinische Seewesen*, ch. xxii. vol. ii.; Heyd, *Commerce du Levant*, etc.

Surely Mr. Herbert Fisher in his *Mediæval Empire*, vol. ii. p. 273, in making the contrast between Constantinople and Tribur as great as that between Versailles and the home of Fergus M'Ivor, somewhat exaggerates the difference. The second Theophano would hardly have endured a mere Highland clansman's lair. When Theophano arrived in Germany to be the bride of Otto II.— *cum innumeris thesaurorum divitiis*—she was regarded as ruining German simplicity by luxury and dress (see Schlumberger, *Basil II.*).

[13] Banduri, *Imperium Orientale*, 1711, and Ducange, *Constantinopolis Christiana*, Gyllius, and Busbecq, give us some idea of Con-

stantinople in its wreck after the sack of the Latins. Labarte's elaborate work, *Le Palais Impérial*, gives a wonderful picture of the extent and splendour of the Sacred Palace, and see Paspates' *Palaces*, now translated by Dr. Metcalfe (1893).

Gibbon's description of the city was an astonishing act of imagination in one who could only consult books, and those antiquated and imperfect. Those who have never beheld Constantinople should study Salzenberg's grand work on S. Sophia and other churches, and the new account of the Walls of Constantinople in Prof. van Millingen's recent work.

[14] *Corpus Scriptorum Historiæ Byzantinæ*; Codinus, *De Ædificiis Con. de Signis*; Paulus Silentiarius, *Descriptio S. Sophiæ*, translated in Salzenberg.

See Bury's *Gibbon* ii. App. v. p. 546, and consult van Millingen's *Walls*, and his introduction to Murray's *Handbook*.

[15] *Early Travels in Palestine*. T. Wright. 1868. And see Gibbon, ch. lx. vi. 393.

"As they passed along, they gazed with admiration on the capital of the East, or as it should seem, of the earth, rising from her seven hills and towering over the continents of Europe and Asia. The swelling domes and lofty spires of 500 palaces and churches were gilded by the sun and reflected in the waters; the walls were crowded with soldiers and spectators, whose numbers they beheld, of whose temper they were ignorant; and each heart was chilled by the reflection that, since the beginning of the world, such an enterprise had never been undertaken by such a handful of warriors" (see Villehardouin, *Histoire de la Conquête*). All this was true enough in the thirteenth century. In the tenth or even in the eleventh it would have proved a very different adventure.

[16] Hodgkin, *Italy and her Invaders*, v. 267.

Bury, *Later Roman Empire*, ii. 313.

Dr. Hodgkin's exhaustive work bears frequent witness to this truth. See his accounts of the immense superiority of the armies of Belisarius and of Narses, iv. 5-7, v. 40, 166. Also the various proposals for matrimonial alliances between Charles and the Imperial family, viii. 12, 210, and the embassies to and from Aachen and Byzantium, viii. 245.

[17] The persistence of Otto the Great in demanding a Byzantine alliance, in spite of rebuffs and difficulties, was a striking fact. It is clear that he regarded it as of great importance to have formal recognition of his claim to empire.

Looked at from the point of view of Byzantine history, the coronation of Charles in 800 was an event of local interest which did not vitally concern the Empire of the Bosphorus. Neither its subjects nor the Orthodox Church were at all shaken or troubled by it. The establishment of the Holy Roman Empire by Otto and his dynasty in the tenth century was a much more decisive change. It notified to the world that there were two co-existent and permanent empires, one of which was Greek, and only Roman by courtesy.

[18] These various forms of modern civilisation are brought out in Rambaud's *L'empire Grec*, Krause's *Byzantiner des Mittelalters*, and Schlumberger's *Empereur Byzantin*. See also Bayet and Heyd.

Perhaps the most curiously modern effect in all the contemporary Byzantine authors is to be found in Constantine Porphyrogenitus' own work, *De Ceremoniis*. His tone is that of a James I., or a Louis XIV. (in his dotage) explaining the niceties of Court etiquette to crowds of obsequious functionaries with all the absolute serenity of supreme power.

The modern character of Constantinople comes out in Sir Henry Pottinger's picturesque romance, *Blue and Green*, 1879, a tale of old Constantinople in the age of Justinian. The Court of Theophilus or Monomachus was far more modern still.

[19] Compare the European coinage of the eighth, ninth, and tenth centuries with the Byzantine as given by Schlumberger and Sabatier. All the emblems of sovereignty are borrowed and paraded. The eternal ball and cross of western sovereignty may be seen in the right hand of the Archangel in the noble Ivory of our British Museum of the early Byzantine epoch, with its Greek epigraph, "Lord receive thy servant, though thou knowest his transgressions." Compare the sovereigns and emperors on Byzantine and in Teutonic illuminations.

Mr. Freeman in his *Norman Conquest*, vol. i., 62-70, and Appendix C., has some interesting remarks on the "Imperial supremacy of the West Saxon Kings." He inclines to think that their use of imperial forms and titles was only in part imitative, and was a *bona fide* claim to rank above kingship. That may be true of such terms as *Basileus, Cæsar, imperator, monarchus*. But when we find Saxon princelets calling themselves *primicerius, archon, pacificus, invictissimus, gloriosus*, and so forth, it is plain that they were borrowing grandiloquent titles.

Charles's formal style, "serenissimus Augustus, crowned of God, great and pacific emperor," and the like, was identical with the Byzantine style. There is something sublime in Charlemagne calling himself pacific.

[20] As we read in Hodgkin's *Italy*, viii. ch. v., and Bryce's *Holy Roman Empire*, ch. iv., Dr. Hodgkin's view of the assumption of the Imperial Crown by Charles, that it was almost forced on him by the Pope, has every evidence in its favour. The empire of Charles had at first more of an ecclesiastical than a purely temporal character. Neither Charles nor his agents saw, or could see, all that the empire became with Hohenstauffens and Hapsburgs. Mr. Fisher has well pointed out in his opening chapter that the Western Empire was very loosely and differently understood down to the coronation of Otto I. in 962.

[21] The modifications in the organisation of the Empire have been thoroughly worked out by Mr. Bury in his two volumes; and he has summarised the results in Appendices to his *Gibbon*, vi. 3, 4, and 5.

There is no example of equal method and adaptation to changed conditions in the organisation of the Western Empire, either in its early Latin or later Teutonic form. The Byzantine Empire was a real *government*, and did not become a *title* until the very end.

[22] The whole of Mr. Oman's chapter on *Byzantine Armies*, bk. iv. A.D. 579-1204, should be studied. He concludes (p. 201):—

"The art of war as it was understood at Constantinople in the tenth century was the only system of real merit existing in the world; no Western nation could have afforded such a training to its officers till the sixteenth, or we may even say the seventeenth century." He goes on to analyse the *Tactics* of Nicephorus Phocas in the tenth century: "it might be used on the Indian north-west frontier to-day, so practical is it."

[23] Bury's *Gibbon*, vi. App. 5.

Schlumberger's *Nicephorus Phocas*, ch. ii. p. 32.

Of this wonderful expedition and conquest of Crete we have the contemporary account of Leo Diaconus in *Corp. Byzant. Histor.*, and the poem of Theodosius the Deacon, in the same volume.

[24] So Luitprand reports in his amusing *Legatio*. Of course we must take much of the witty Bishop's report to be gross exaggeration and flattery of his imperial master. If Otto the Great had believed all the Bishop reported of the barbarism of Byzantium, why did he again risk a rebuff and ultimately win for his son the imperial princess "born in the Purple"?

Luitprand tells us what the words of Nicephorus were as to the sea-power of his empire compared with that of Otto—"nec est in mari domino tuo classium numerus. Navigantium fortitudo mihi soli inest, qui cum classibus aggrediar bello, maritimas eius civitates demoliar, et quae fluminibus sunt vicina, redigam in favillam." Nor was this an empty boast. It reminds one of Cromwell's threat to the Italian princes.

The famous "Greek fire" has been fully discussed by Schlumberger, *Phocas*, ch. ii., and by Bury, ii. 311, 319, and see his *Gibbon*, vi. App. 5. He explains the great varieties of these combustible and explosive compounds, and the modes of using them. One method seems to have been a form of gunpowder ignited to discharge liquid combustibles through some sort of gun. Constantine Porphyrogenitus in his work *De administrando Imperio*, ch. xlviii., calls this τὸ διὰ τῶν σιφώνων ἐκφερόμενον πῦρ ὑγρόν, and says it was invented by Callinicus of Heliopolis in the time of Constantine Pogonatus (*i.e.* seventh century). The Byzantines seem to have reached the point of inventing (1) gunpowder, (2) using its explosion to drive missiles, (3) applying the gunpowder to guns (σίφωνες). Why did they get no farther? Perhaps they were unable to use hard or solid missiles, or to expel the charge beyond a short distance, because they could not make guns strong enough to resist a powerful charge. Their σίφωνες were in fact "Roman candles" and other fireworks. They do not seem to have been effective except at close quarters, to defend walls and on board ships. For these purposes, the "Greek fire" seems to have been quite crushing; and from the seventh to the tenth century, it gave the Byzantine garrisons and warships some such superiority over Saracens and Scythians that gunpowder in modern times gives to civilised nations against barbarians. Consult Oman, *Art of War*, 545-48.

[25] A series of German scholars have collected and edited the post-Justinian Law of the Roman Empire. Zachariae von Lingenthal has published *Collectio Librorum Juris Graeco-Romani ineditorum*, etc., Leipzig, 1852, in which the Isaurian codes and institutes are collected. His *Jus Graeco-Romanum*, Leipzig, 1856, has been translated into French by E. Louth as *Histoire du droit Gréco-Romain*, Paris, 1870. And Montreuil has published *Histoire du droit Byzantin*, 2 vols., Paris, 1843.

The immense collection of the *Basilica* were published by Heimbach, and edited by Zachariae: *Basilicorum Libri LX Gr. et Lat.*, 6 tom., 4to, Leipzig, 1833-70. Also Haubold, *Manuale Basilicorum*, 1819, a collation of Justinian with the later law.

Mr. Bury has treated the post-Justinian law in his chapter on Leo III., ii. 411-420, but his *Later Roman Empire* has not reached the Basilian era. He treats it also in his *Gibbon*, v. App. 11, p. 525, but mainly from the point of view of criminal law.

Mr. Roby, in his *Introduction to the Study of Justinian's Digest*, 1884, pp. ccxli.-ccliv., has touched on this Greco-Roman law. Otherwise English civilians do not seem to have concerned themselves with a branch of Roman law on which foreign jurists have worked for more than two generations.

[26] Savigny's *History of Roman Law in the Middle Ages* (1815-31) was written before the publications of Heimbach and Zachariae, and he does not seem to have paid any attention to the persistence and development of Roman law in the East. He triumphantly proved in his famous work that the Roman law was not absolutely extinct, and he found traces of it in Rome, Ravenna, amongst Lombards, Burgundians, Franks, and Goths. But he is not able to show anything like a *Corpus Juris*, schools of Justinian law, or any systematic treatises down to the rise of the Bolognese school early in the twelfth century. He suggests as a reason for the revival of civil law in Bologna that it was near to Ravenna, which did not cease to belong to the Empire until 751. We may remember that Amalfi and some other Italian seaports remained in Byzantine hands much later, and Byzantine influence in Calabria continued down to the Norman conquest.

[27] Mr. Hodgkin, in his *Italy and its Invaders*, vi., has treated of the Lombard laws, and has noticed those of the Isaurian emperors.

If we turn to these Lombard and Frank codes, or to the Caroline capitularies, or the Saxon laws as collected by Dr. Liebermann, *Gesetze der Angelsachsen* (1899), 4to, we find rude, semi-barbarous penalties and "dooms,"—so much for cutting off a thumb, so much for killing a slave, and the like,—but nothing that could be called a scientific code of civil law. Whilst Ine and Rothari in the seventh century, Alfred and the Carlings in the ninth century, were exacting fines and promulgating penalties for violence, the Byzantine world was continuously ordered by working versions of Justinian's law. Down to the time of Cnut or the Franconian emperors there is nothing in Western Europe that, as a scientific code of law, can be compared with the *Basilica*.

As Mr. Fisher well reminds us (*The Mediæval Empire*, i. 156, ch. iv.), there was no knowledge of Roman law in Germany until much later.

[28] *Basilicorum Libri LX.* (Heimbach and Zachariae), vol. i. p. xxi. This fine preface is worthy of Justinian himself, and certainly contains an unanswerable criticism on the redaction of the *Corpus Juris*. It is obvious that the Basilian editors do not cite the *Corpus Juris* direct from the Latin text. They use translations, summaries, commentaries, and handbooks which had multiplied during three centuries. How strikingly does such a fact witness to the persistence of civil law in the East as compared with its hibernation in the West—a dormant state which till the time of Savigny was thought to be death. Contrast with the rude laws of Franks and Saxons the titles of the *Procheiron* of Basil. These run thus:— Sponsalia—Marriage—Dower—Property of Husband and Wife—Dissolution of Marriage—Gift—Revocation—Sale—Lease—Pledge—Bailment—Partnership—Testament—Emancipation—Disinheriting—Legacies—Tutors. Here we are in the region of scientific jurisprudence.

[29] The great work of Salzenberg, *Alt-christliche Baudenkmale*, with its excellent reproductions, should be studied by those who have never seen Constantinople. A scientific and historical account of the great church of the Holy Wisdom ("the fairest church in all the world"—Sir J. Mandeville) has been published by W. R.

Lethaby and Harold Swainson (London, 1894, 4to). These enthusiasts—the one historical scholar, the other architect—declare that "Sancta Sophia is the most interesting building on the world's surface"—"one of the four great pinnacles of architecture"— "the supreme monument of the Christian cycle." Their work contains references to the principal authorities for the history and antiquities of the building. See also Ferguson, *History of Architecture*, vol. ii. (Byzantine Architecture); Bury, *Later Roman Empire*, ii. 40-54; and E. Corroyer, *L'Architecture Romaine*, and Bayet, *L'Art Byzantin*.

According to Melchior de Vogüé, *La Syrie Centrale*, the arch supported by the free column may be found of a date earlier than that of Diocletian. If he is right, the *praetorium* of Mousmieh, built by Egnatius Fuscus, A.D. 160-169, under Marcus Aurelius and Lucius Verus, has a definite example of the free column supporting an arch. A column engaged in a wall and bearing a vault was familiar enough in Roman baths and basilicas of the second century. It must be doubtful if Diocletian's palace at Spalato really saw the first invention of this supreme discovery in the art of building. See Freeman, *Essays*, 3rd series, and *Architectural Sketches*.

Fossati's *Agia Sofia*, with chromo-lithographs, gives some suggestion of the colour of the interior and of the general position of this sublime temple.

[30] If we accept the account given by Lanciani (*Ruins and Excavations of Ancient Rome*, 1897, pp. 476-488) and other topographers as to the true date of the Pantheon as we see it, and its relation to the famous inscription on the pediment in front— M·AGRIPPA·L·F·COS·TERTIUM·FECIT. It had always seemed to be a puzzle why the Pantheon, with its marvellous dome, was not imitated and followed for a century and a half, if it were really built so early as B.C. 27. If the true date of the Pantheon be A.D. 125, it belongs to the era of the mighty domes and hemicycles of the second century, and is not so inconceivably premature and solitary in the evolution of Roman architecture.

[31] It seems impossible to study the works of De Vogüé, Texier, and travellers and archæologists in Asia, copied and noted in Ferguson's works, without coming to a definite conclusion as to

the great *influence* of S. Sophia and Byzantine building on the whole East. The modifications of Byzantine types, the immediate source of the influence and the precise dates and channels of intercourse, are complicated problems. Syrian, Armenian, Persian, and Russian styles have their own characteristics. The decisive fact is the general impression produced on the Eastern world by the grandest, most colossal, and most beautiful of all the dome-plus-arch buildings in the world.

[32] Labarte's great work, *Histoire des Arts industriels au moyen âge*, 4 vols. 8vo, 1864, with its illustrative plates, gives a complete résumé of the progress of the decorative arts, from the capture of Rome to the Renaissance. In each case he makes the arrival of the Greek artists in Italy, owing to the Iconoclast persecution in the eighth century, the critical epoch. He has surveyed the history of the arts in turn—sculpture, metal-work, jewelry, enamels, ivories, and illuminated painting, completely establishing the priority and stimulating influence of the Byzantine schools for the early epochs from the sixth to the eleventh centuries. The result is stated summarily in his smaller work, now translated, Labarte, *Handbook of the Arts of the Middle Ages*, 1855, pp. 3 and 17.

The school of Constantinople was in the tenth century the source from which Italy and Germany borrowed artists. The famous *Pala d' oro* of S. Mark's at Venice was ordered by the Doge Orseolo from Constantinople (A.D. 991). The gates of *S. Paolo fuori le mura* at Rome were ordered by Hildebrand from the same school.

Labarte's beautiful reproductions in colours are particularly useful for the illuminated manuscripts. The Vienna Manuscript, painted for Juliana Anicia in the sixth century, is almost classical, not inferior to some Pompeian wall-paintings. The manuscript of Gregory of Nazianzus in the *Bibliothèque Nationale* of Paris, executed in the ninth century for Basil I., is magnificent. Others in Paris are the *Psalms* of the tenth century, and the *Gospel* executed for Nicephorus Phocas, and a manuscript is in the Library of S. Mark's of the date of Basil II. (976). These paintings in design, colour, and drawing are equal to good Italian work of the fifteenth century.

[33] Mosaic decoration (from late Greek μουσεῖον) has been treated in a useful monograph by Canon Venables in *Dictionary of Christian*

Antiquities. The existing mosaic pictures in S. Sophia and other churches at Constantinople and at Thessalonica are as grand as any wall-paintings of any period. That the mosaics of Ravenna, Rome, Venice, Magna Graecia, and Palermo, all anterior to the twelfth century, have a Byzantine origin, or were executed by the aid of the Byzantine school, is obvious both from external and internal evidence. Consult Labarte, *u.s.*, also Ch. Diehl's *L'Art Byzantin dans l'Italie Méridionale*, Paris, 1894.

He has proved that the revival of mosaic art in the eleventh century was accomplished under Byzantine influence—"the incontestable superiority of the Byzantine artists made them the educators of Italy." Extant Italian works at Torcello, Venice, Grotta Ferrata, Monte Cassino, S. Angelo-in-Formis, with their Greek lettering and symbols, amply establish this. The fact that Roman lettering is found in Italy with Greek types, is no evidence against a Byzantine origin; though the presence of Greek letters and types is conclusive on the other side.

See Frothingham, *American Journal of Archæology*, vol. ix., 1894. During the eighth century Rome was full of Greek monks, ecclesiastics, and artists. In 867 Lazarus, a prominent Byzantine painter, was sent to Rome—"pictoriae artis nimie eruditi" (*Liber Pontific.*). San Prassede at Rome, and S. Mark's at Venice, were executed by Greek artists. The bronze doors of Amalfi, Salerno, Ravello, and St. Paul's at Rome were obviously of Byzantine design. The rough drawings of the gates of St. Paul's in d'Agincourt, taken before the fire of 1823, are visibly Greek. And the *pala d' oro* enamels of St. Mark's at Venice exhibit the same type. Both were ordered from Constantinople.

The mediæval mosaics of Europe show one type, and one set of *motifs*, and down to the fifteenth century these seem to have had a common origin in the Byzantine world.

[34] Labarte (*Histoire des Arts*, vol. i.) treats of the art of ivory-carving, and his sumptuous plates give an idea of the state of the art in the Byzantine period. He regards the noble Michael of our Museum to be of the age of Justinian. Several of the early diptychs he reproduces have the character of Western work as late as the fourteenth century. The South Kensington Museum contains numerous caskets and diptychs, original and copies, of which the *Handbook* by W. Maskell gives a useful account. The

Veroli casket in that collection, if really mediæval, is proof that the classical sense of form did not entirely expire with Polytheism.

[35] Very fine Byzantine illuminations before the twelfth century are not numerous, and none of the best seem to be in England. But the reproductions given by Labarte, by Silvestre and Champollion, *Universal Palæography*, by Westwood, *Palæographia Sacra Pictoria*, and by N. Humphreys, *Illuminated Books of the Middle Ages*, show grand examples of the early Byzantine school in Venice, Vienna, Rome, and Paris. Silvestre (*Paléographie Universelle*, Paris, 1841) reproduces some of these. The Byzantine miniatures of our British Museum, if not equal to the best abroad, are greatly superior in drawing and composition to the purely Western paintings down to the thirteenth or fourteenth centuries. The calligraphy of the Greeks does not equal that of the best Irish, French, and German schools, and the Greeks eschew the fantastic borders and initial letters which are the main features of the Northern, especially of the Irish schools, reaching their acme in the Book of Kells. But in dignity of pose, in drawing, in force of expression, some of the best Byzantine paintings anterior to the eleventh century have never been surpassed at any period of the art of miniature. From that epoch it rapidly declined, and became at last utterly conventional and mechanical.

Much light was thrown on the history of Byzantine art by M. Didron's discovery of the painter's handbook in the hands of the monks of Mount Athos. The ἑρμηνεία τῆς Ζωγραφικῆς, translated and published as *Manuel d'iconographie Chrétienne*, 1845, is said by Didron to be as old as the eleventh century. Its general instructions may have been much older. It contains first, elaborate practical rules for the painter, and next it gives the *motifs* of some hundreds of designs for compositions, representing every incident in Old and New Testament and in Sacred Hagiology. Here, in fact, in an old monkish practice-book, are the types of sacred art as we find it in sculpture, mosaic, fresco, metal, and illuminated work from the sixth to the sixteenth century, and from Syria to Ireland, throughout the Christian world. The scheme which these Greek monks used traditionally to represent the Last Supper is essentially that which Leonardo and Raffaelle adopted. The scheme of their Last Judgment is that of a thousand mosaics, frescoes, carvings, and illuminations throughout Europe, and indeed the same as

Michael Angelo painted in the Sistine Chapel. It would be difficult to find, down to the 16th century, any representation of a sacred incident in any form of art in Europe, of which the type is not given in this old Greek ἑρμηνεία. Christian art, like Christian theology and Catholic ritual, was formed throughout the Middle Ages out of a Greek *matrix*—Eastern, though not Byzantine specially, until the advance of the Crescent forced Greek Christendom back to the Bosphorus.

[36] See Francisque-Michel, *Recherches sur le commerce, la fabrication, et l'usage des étoffes de soie, d'or, et d'argent en l'Occident pendant le Moyen Age.* 2 vols. Paris, 1852.

The manufacture of silk embroidery was an eminently Greek industry, derived from Ptolemaic Alexandria, and the Empire became its emporium and seat. It was carried to wonderful elaboration. The robe of a senator had embroidered on it no less than six hundred figures picturing the entire life of Christ. The famous Dalmatic of the Vatican is drawn in Schlumberger's *Nicephorus Phocas*, p. 301. It is a wonderful work of embroidery. These were manufactured at Byzantium and other Greek cities and sent all over the West. William of Tyre records the mass of robes—*tapetibus et holosericis*—found by the Crusaders at the sack of Antioch in 1098, as does Villehardouin of the prodigious quantity of samite found at Constantinople at the sack of 1204. During the Middle Ages quantities of these embroideries were sent to kings and nobles and greatly esteemed One of the stuffs was called *imperialis*.

[37] On the subject of Byzantine literature consult the great work of Karl Krumbacher, *Geschichte der Byzantinischen Literatur*, 2nd cd., by Ehrbuch and Gelzer (Munich, 1897). This elaborate work, in some 1200 pp., reviews the whole course of Byzantine literature from A.D. 527 to 1453. It is a field whereon English scholars seem never to have touched. It is no doubt probable that these numerous works are now as nearly as possible worthless, and few living Englishmen are likely to devote their time to them. But as a fact in general history, their production has great interest. Some of the Byzantine historians rise above that dead level of dullness with which they are usually dismissed. Krumbacher will not allow that even the Byzantine poetry is absolutely barren. The

Silentiary's poem on S. Sophia is unquestionably ingenious, and even the iambics of George Pisides and of Theodosius the Deacon, are less barbarous than the Latin contemporary effusions. I suppose some worse verses are annually sent up to the examiners in our universities. Even modern laureates do not always produce high poetry.

I cannot speak from knowledge on the subject of Music. But I gather from the learned article with that title in Smith's *Dictionary of Christian Antiquities*, that "for the first thousand years of the Christian era, the antique Greek system of music was adopted, with but few alterations, and those chiefly modifications of the compass of the scale and of the notation." "During the first six centuries of the Christian era the Greek musical notation was in universal use." The great change was not made until the eleventh century by Guido of Arezzo.

The Byzantine court maintained a regular band of musicians and organs. Leo the Isaurian, and his son Copronymus, encouraged music, and are said to have given public concerts. Copronymus sent to Pippin the first organ that ever reached Western Europe (Bury, ii. 462).

[38] It is impossible for modern scholarship to ignore all that it owes to the laborious lexicographers, scholiasts, and anecdote-mongers of Byzantium, although our own generation has almost forgotten how the knowledge of the Greek language and literature has been preserved to Western Europe. Amongst other of its debts to Mediæval Greece we might note the various Greek words in modern speech which are derived through Mediæval Latin, French, or Italian, not being new coinage such as *telegram, enteritis,* or *atlas*. The words of official, artistic, ecclesiastical, and ceremonial usage derived through Low Latin, or *lingua franca*, are very numerous, and point to a borrowing of practice—almanac, policy (of assurance), catholic, chemist, dogma, tactics, anthem, basilica, cemetery, diploma, doxology, pope, priest, psalm, dimity, heresy, hermit, laity, litany, mosaic, pandect, parchment, piastre, patriot, patriarch, pragmatic, protocol, samite, syndic, synod, piazza, torso, catapult, bottle, butler, encaustic, hierarchy, catacomb. Some of these words were, no doubt, in use before the transfer of the seat of empire to Byzantium, but their constant usage in the Greek world has led to their general adoption in Europe.

[39] NEANDER, *Church History*, passim.
MILMAN, *Latin Christianity*, vols. i. and ii.
NEALE, *Holy Eastern Church*.
HODGKIN, *Italy and Her Invaders*, vols. iv. vi. viii.
BURY, *Later Roman Empire*, vols. i. and ii.
"Controversies" in Smith's *Dictionary of Christian Antiquities;*
"Lives" in Smith's *Dictionary of Christian Biography*.

[40] The Iconoclastic movement down to Irene has been efficiently treated by Bury in his second volume. But it outlasted the reaction of that Empress. A sketch of the whole movement is given in the *Dictionary of Christian Antiquities* under "Images." The interesting and picturesque narratives of Gibbon and of Milman hardly do justice to the long persistence of the Iconoclastic movement, and the enthusiastic support which it must have received from the martial Asiatic portions of the Empire. It was a far deeper and more national effort than the arbitrary ideas of such imperial reformers as Tzar Peter or Francis II.

[41] The jealousy of Old Rome for New Rome began from the first. Claudian and Sidonius in the 5th century are full of it, see Dill, *Roman Society in the 5th Century*, p. 283, etc. Under Gregory and successive Popes, this Roman jealousy turned into theological hatred and contempt, as Fisher remarks (*Mediæval Empire*, i. 19), "the whole influence of the Latin Church was exerted to preach a misleading view of historical continuity." The partisans of Latin Church and of Western Empire vied with each other to the same end, whenever Pope or Empire were not beset by rivals and enemies nearer home. It still remains the task of historical scholarship to remove much of the misconception which still lingers in the mind of the public.